Who God says I am

BOYS EDITION

WHO GOD SAYS I AM: BOYS EDITION

ISBN - 978-1-7351373-2-2

Published by In His Grace Ministries LLC

Book website: www.inhisgrace.com/product/who-i-am-in-christ-boys-edition/

Dedication

Even though, my son, you are hardly a little boy anymore at 22 years of age; I wanted to dedicate this book to you and let you know that God has a love for you that no one else has. Keep close to your heart who you are and who's you are. Remember how very important you are to everyone who knows you. I am so proud of the man you have become and continue to be. I love you, son!

I am Confident

"But blessed is the one who trusts in the Lord, whose confidence is in Him."
Jeremiah 17:7

I am Strong

"I can do all this through Him who gives me strength."
Philippians 4:13

I am Loved

"And so we know and rely on the love God has for us. God is love. Whoever lives in love lives in God, and God in them."
1 John 4:16

I am Wise

"The fear of the Lord is the beginning of wisdom, and knowledge of the Holy One is understanding."
Proverbs 9:10

I am
Self-controlled

"Rather, he must be hospitable, one who loves what is good, who is self-controlled, upright, holy and disciplined."
Titus 1:8

I am Fearless

"I sought the Lord, and He answered me; He delivered me from all my fears."
Psalm 34:4

I am
Complete

"being confident of this, that He who began a good work in you will carry it on to completion until the day of Christ Jesus."
Philippians 1:6

I am His Friend

"Greater love has no one than this: to lay down one's life for one's friends."
John 15:13

I am Chosen

"You did not choose me, but I chose you and appointed you so that you might go and bear fruit—fruit that will last—and so that whatever you ask in my name the Father will give you."
John 15:16

"Yet to all who did receive Him, to those who believed in His name, He gave the right to become children of God—
John 1:12

Remember who

God

says you are

I am

Self-Controlled

Confident

Strong

Wise

Loved

Fearless

Friend

Chosen

THE SON
OF A *KING*

Complete

and so much more...

Milton Keynes UK
Ingram Content Group UK Ltd.
UKHW052357010823
426181UK00003B/7